Lift and Shift

Toys That Build

SCHOLASTIC

Conceived and produced by Weldon Owen Pty Ltd,
59–61 Victoria Street, McMahons Point,
Sydney, NSW 2060, Australia

International Sales Office: kristiner@weldonowen.com.au

Library of Congress Cataloging-in-Publication Data

Scott, Janine

  Lift and shift: toys that build / by Janine Scott

ISBN 13: 978-0-545-37245-9
ISBN 10: 0-545-37245-3

A CIP catalog record for this book is available from the
Library of Congress.

Published in the United States by
Scholastic Inc.
557 Broadway
New York, New York 10012
www.scholastic.com

11 12 13 14 15 16 17 18
10 9 8 7 6 5 4 3 2 1

Printed by Toppan Leefung in China

The paper used in the manufacture of this book
is sourced from wood grown in sustainable forests.
It complies with the Environmental Management
System Standard ISO 14001:2004

Weldon Owen Pty Ltd
Managing Director Kay Scarlett
Publisher Corinne Roberts
Creative Director Sue Burk

Managing Editors Lynette Evans, Janine Scott
Designer Karen Sagovac
Images Manager Trucie Henderson
Design Assistant Emily Spencer
Production Director Todd Rechner
Production and Pre-press Controller Mike Crowton
Production Controller Lisa Conway

Photographs: BigStock 3br; 14b; 15r; 17t. **Corbis** 20-21
Dreamstime cover; 3r; 4-5b; 6-7b; 7t; 8-9bg; 12-13b;
13br; 16-17b; 18-19c; 19r; 20-21b; 22tl, tr, br; 22-23t; 23b
28bc. **iStockphoto.com** 2-3t; 6-7b; 10b; 10-11bg, b, c;
11r; 12-13c; 13r, b; 14cl; 14-15bg, c; 16-17bg; 18-19c, r;
20-21bc; 21r, b; 22-23t, b; 23c; 24b; 25br; 26bl. **Library o**
Congress 4-5bg; 6-7bg; 24-25bg. **Shutterstock** 5r; 13tr.

All other photographs and illustrations
© Weldon Owen Pty Ltd

A WELDON OWEN PRODUCTION

CONTENTS

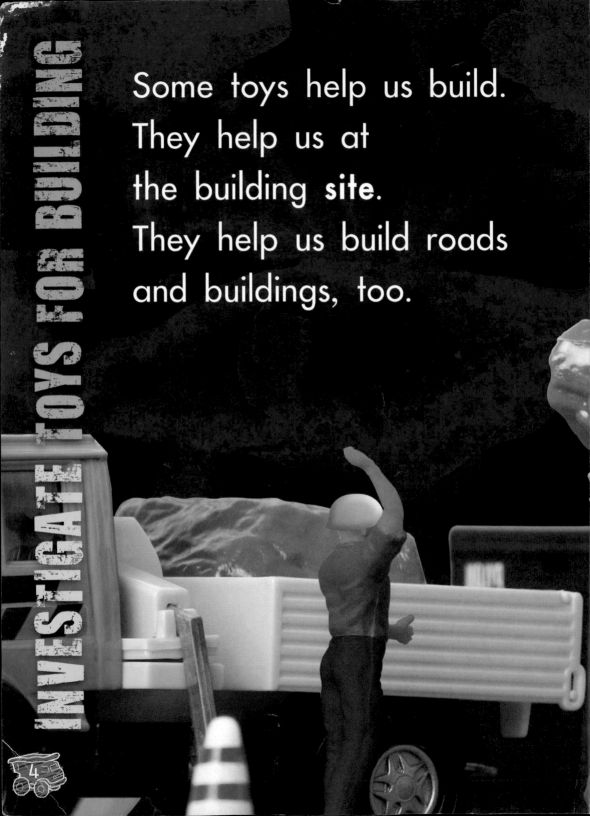

Some toys help us build.
They help us at
the building **site**.
They help us build roads
and buildings, too.

How do toys help us build?

Toys that help us build
do different jobs.
Diggers dig holes.
Cranes lift things.
Trucks carry
heavy things.

Crane

Digger

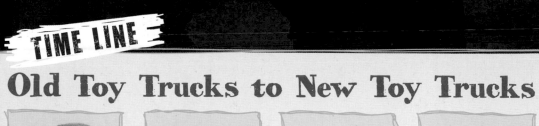

Old Toy Trucks to New Toy Trucks

1930s ➤ 1940s ➤ 1960s ➤ Today

Truck

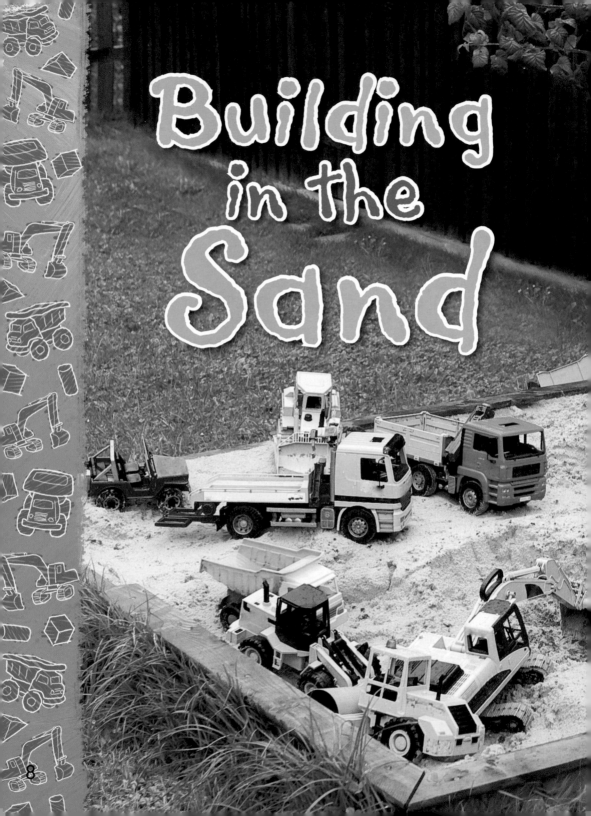

Building in the Sand

Here is a sandbox.
There are lots of different toys
in the sand.

Which toys help us build?

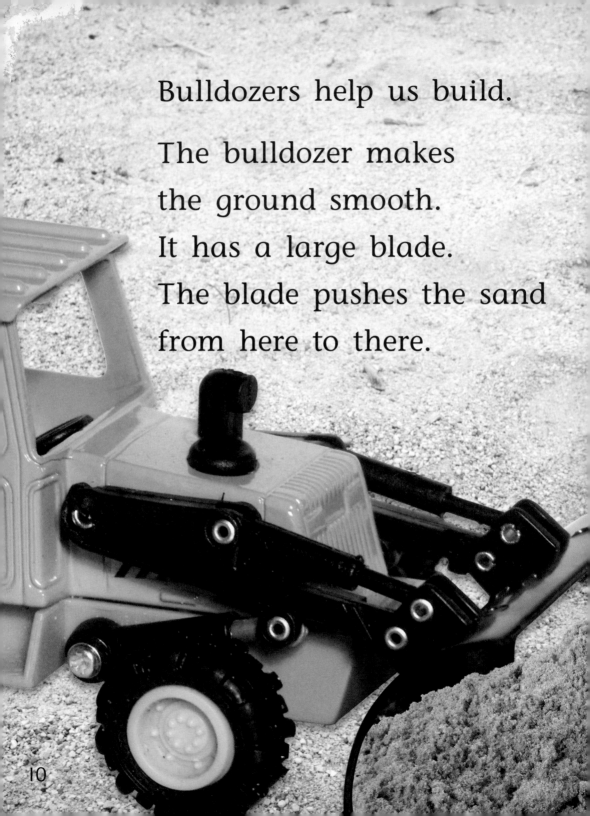

Bulldozers help us build.

The bulldozer makes
the ground smooth.
It has a large blade.
The blade pushes the sand
from here to there.

Blade lifting sand

Blade

The blade on a bulldozer lifts sand, soil, rocks, and **rubble**. The blade can move up and down.

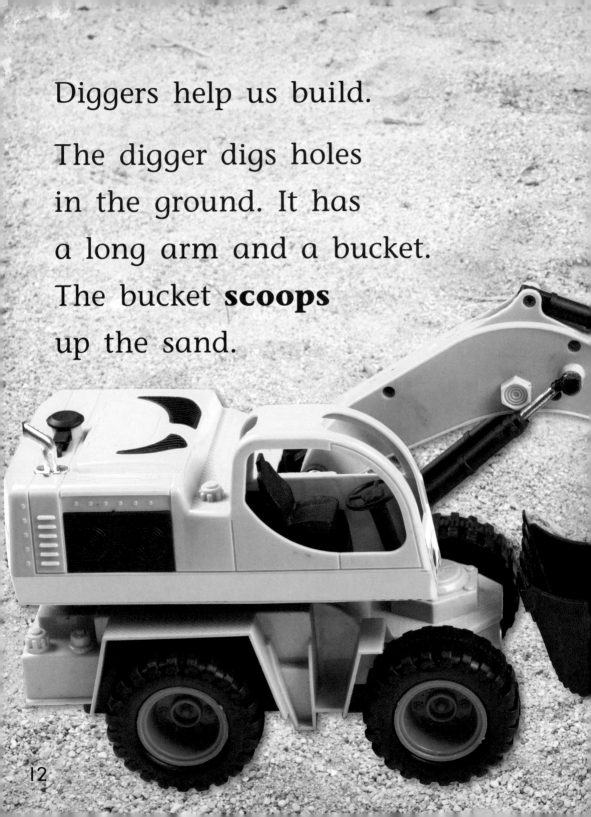

Diggers help us build.

The digger digs holes
in the ground. It has
a long arm and a bucket.
The bucket **scoops**
up the sand.

On the Move

Scoop, scoop, scoop.

Arm

Bucket

Some toys for building move on wheels.

Some toys for building move on tracks.

Dump trucks help us build.

The dump truck has a huge body. It moves sand from one place to another.

Body

The body **tilts** up.
The sand falls
to the ground.

Up goes the body.
Up, up, up.

Down goes the sand.
Down, down, down.

Rollers help us build.

The heavy drum rolls out bumps in the ground. It makes the **surface** flat.

Some toy rollers have two heavy drums.

Drum

Roll, roll, roll.

Cranes help us build.

The crane has a hook
for carrying things.
It lifts things and moves
them from place to place.

Pulley

Cable

Hook

Up goes the crane.

Up, up, up.

Boom

Up and Down

A crane has a long arm called a boom. A **pulley** moves the cable and hook up and down.

Forklift trucks help us lift things, too.

19

Friends help us build.

They dig in the sand.
They drive the machines.
They make toys lift and shift.

They do a good job!

21

Lifting Parts

These new toy cranes pull up large blue pipes. Pulleys help them lift things.

Shifting Parts

This old toy tractor can push and pull heavy things.

Spinning Parts

This new toy concrete mixer has a spinning drum. The spinning drum helps mix sand and water.

Grabbing Parts

This new toy loader picks up blocks. A big claw helps it grab things.

Machines on the Move

How do these toys lift and shift?

Dumping Parts

This old skip truck lifts and shifts a large yellow skip. Real skips hold rubble and other things.

CONNECT WITH TOYS FOR BUILDING

We can build with blocks. We can make a house with blocks. We can make a fence with blocks. We can use many different shapes.

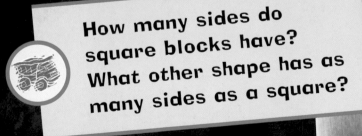

How many sides do square blocks have? What other shape has as many sides as a square?

Which shapes are good for the roof of a house?

Which shapes are good for the sides of a house?

pulley – a wheel and a rope that lifts or moves things

rubble – bits of broken stone or brick

scoop – to dig

site – the place where something is built

surface – the top part of something

tilt – to lean

Building site

Some machines help us build. Different machines do different jobs. Diggers help prepare the building site by digging holes.

Book
Zobel, Derek.
Diggers
(Blastoff!).
Scholastic Inc., 2009.

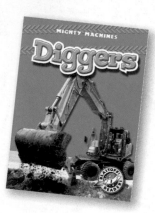

Web Site
http://www.bobthebuilder.com/usa/
games_racing_mazes.asp

Toy digger